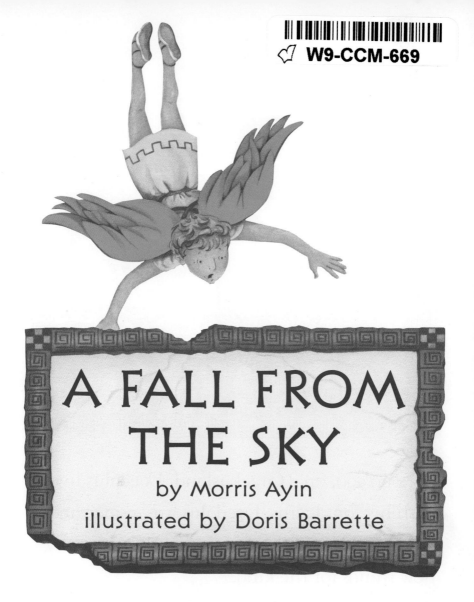

A FALL FROM THE SKY

by Morris Ayin

illustrated by Doris Barrette

◟Harcourt

Orlando   Boston   Dallas   Chicago   San Diego

Visit *The Learning Site!*

www.harcourtschool.com

Long ago, on a Greek island, Daedalus lived with his son, Icarus. Daedalus was a smart man who worked with his hands. He created many new things for the king.

One day, Daedalus made the king very angry. "I will kill that man and his son!" the king shouted.

The king sent men to capture Daedalus and Icarus. They looked and looked but could not find them. The two were hiding in a cave.

"I will wait," the king said. "The only way they can get off this island is to fly. That is a feat that even Daedalus cannot do!"

The king did not know that Daedalus did
plan to fly! In his cave, Daedalus was making
a set of wings for himself.

First, he made a frame of wood. Then, he
rubbed wax all over the frame to make it
sticky. Last, he stuck thousands of feathers
onto the frame.

Icarus stood and watched his father work.
He saw how beautiful the wings looked when
they were done.

"They look like the wings of a bird!"
Icarus cried.

Daedalus then made a set of wings for his son.

"Now we both have wings," Daedalus said. "We can both fly to another land. With luck, the people there will be kind and show us hospitality. We will be safe from the king."

Daedalus was very smart. Before flying, he made a plan with Icarus.

"We will fly at night," Daedalus said. "I will lead the way. If we cannot stay together, fly to the place I have marked on this map. I will meet you there."

That night, Daedalus and Icarus left their cave. Quickly they walked to the top of a tall cliff. They looked around to make sure no spectators would see them.

"I have one last thing to tell you," Daedalus
said to Icarus. "Fly fast but not too high."

Daedalus then restated his warning. "Do not
fly too high, Icarus. You will not be safe if you
fly too high."

Just then the wind blew. Daedalus jumped off the cliff. He flapped his wings and flew in the dark.

Icarus then jumped and flew. "This is so much fun!" Icarus cried. "I feel like a bird!"

As they had planned, Daedalus led the
way. He flew fast and steady in a line.

For a while, Icarus stayed close to his
father. Then he wanted to have some fun.

"I can catch up with my father later,"
he said.

What a good time Icarus had with his new wings!

For a long time, he refused to stop. He didn't see how far Daedalus had gone.

At last Icarus said, "Now I must catch up with my father."

Icarus flew fast but could not find Daedalus. He began to worry. The sky was so dark. Where was the place to meet his father? Which was the right way to get there?

Icarus flew all night. In the pre-dawn light, he looked all over for Daedalus, with no luck. Now he began to worry even more.

"It will be day soon," he said. "What if a hunter sees me and thinks I am a bird? He may try to shoot me with an arrow!"

The sun rose. Soon it was high in the sky.

"I know I shouldn't fly too high," Icarus said. "But I must take the chance. If I fly higher, maybe I will see my father."

Up and up Icarus flew. As he got closer to the sun, the wax on his wings melted. Icarus flapped hard but could no longer fly. Down and down he fell, into the deep sea! No hero or heroine was there to save him.

Poor Icarus! He had flown too close to the sun!